Fabulous FASHIONS of the 1950s

FELICIA
LOWENSTEIN
NIVEN

Fabulous FASHIONS of the DECADES

Enslow Publishers, Inc.
40 Industrial Road
Box 398
Berkeley Heights, NJ 07922
USA
http://www.enslow.com

Library of Congress Cataloging-in-Publication Data
Niven, Felicia Lowenstein.
    Fabulous fashions of the 1950s / Felicia Lowenstein Niven.
       p. cm. — (Fabulous fashions of the decades)
    Fabulous fashions of the nineteen fifties
    Includes bibliographical references and index.
    Summary: "Discusses the fashions of the 1950s, including women's and men's clothing and hairstyles,
      accessories, trends and fads, and world events that influenced the fashion"—Provided by publisher.
    ISBN 978-0-7660-3825-7
    1. Fashion—History—20th century—Juvenile literature. 2. Fashion design—History—20th century—
    Juvenile literature. 3. Lifestyle—History—20th century—Juvenile literature. 4. Nineteen fifties—
    Juvenile literature. I. Title. II. Title: Fabulous fashions of the nineteen fifties.
      TT504.N575 2011
      746.9'2—dc22
                  2010014587

Paperback ISBN: 978-1-59845-278-5

Printed in the United States of America

052011 Lake Book Manufacturing, Inc., Melrose Park, IL

10 9 8 7 6 5 4 3 2 1

To Our Readers: We have done our best to make sure all Internet Addresses in this book were active and appropriate when we went to press. However, the author and the publisher have no control over and assume no liability for the material available on those Internet sites or on other Web sites they may link to. Any comments or suggestions can be sent by e-mail to comments@enslow.com or to the address on the back cover.

Every effort has been made to locate all copyright holders of material used in this book. If any errors or omissions have occurred, corrections will be made in future editions of this book.

♻ Enslow Publishers, Inc., is committed to printing our books on recycled paper. The paper in every book contains 10% to 30% post-consumer waste (PCW). The cover board on the outside of each book contains 100% PCW. Our goal is to do our part to help young people and the environment too!

Illustration Credits: Advertising Archive/courtesy Everett Collection, p. 4; AP Images, p. 41; AP Images/Matty Zimmerman, p. 20; Camerique/ClassicStock/Everett Collection, p. 39; © ClassicStock/Alamy, p. 17; courtesy Everett Collection, pp. 1, 6, 10, 13, 14, 26, 36, 40; Dover Publications, Inc./Sears®, pp. 5, 8, 11, 15, 18, 22, 25, 27, 28, 29, 32, 35; Lanks/ClassicStock/Everett Collection, p. 33; Library of Congress, pp. 42–44; Shutterstock, pp. 37, 46; © Trinity Mirror/Mirrorpix/Alamy, p. 30; © 20th Century-Fox Film Corp. All Rights Reserved./Everett Collection, p. 23.

Cover Illustration: courtesy Everett Collection (dark-haired woman).

Contents

The 1950s

Introduction: Wild and Crazy Fads 5

1 Hairstyles 11

2 Women's Styles and Fashion 15

3 Men's Styles and Fashion 22

4 Accessories...............................27

5 Fads and Trends.........................32

6 Pop Culture..............................37

Timeline 42

Glossary 45

Further Reading
(Books and Internet Addresses) 46

Index 47

The 1950s

A 1950s ad for General Electric® shows a family having a great time putting groceries away inside their brand-new, roomy refrigerator. The wife performs her chores in a dress and high heels, not exactly the right footwear for housework!

"Here's the __roomy__ G-E Refrigerator my family won't outgrow!"

Wild and Crazy Fads

What do you want to be when you grow up? If you said a housewife, you'd be like the girls in the 1950s. Back then, housework was the job of the woman while the man went to work.

If you think that's crazy, wait until you hear what women wore to do housework. Here's a hint: it wasn't exactly the most comfortable. If you guessed dresses, you're right! Of course, the dresses weren't as fancy as the ones on television. Actresses who played housewives wore really full skirts and high heels!

It was part of the feminine look. Fifties fashion focused on female curves. Tiny waists showed off full hips. Rows of petticoats created fuller skirts. By contrast, the pencil skirt showed natural curves.

Sheer blouses were especially popular with teenage girls. They wore lacy slips underneath, which were seen through the fabric.

American actress Grace Kelly (1929–1982), who married the Prince of Monaco in 1956, wears an elegant fur stole. But you didn't have to be royalty or a celebrity to pull off this look!

Introduction: Wild and Crazy Fads

These types of outfits worked for home and for school. They got even dressier for going out. Women dressed to entertain at home. They dressed for the theater. They even wore hats and gloves to look more polished.

By the end of the decade, women started dressing a little more casually. It seemed that men weren't the only ones who wore the pants in the family!

Save the Pants for Home

You probably don't think twice about wearing jeans to school. But that would not happen in the 1950s. Girls wore skirts or dresses to school every day. They would save their pants to wear at home when they were just hanging around. They did not call them jeans, either. They were known as dungarees.

Women's pants had a notable difference from their male counterparts. They zipped on the side. It was considered more proper than zipping up the front.

Go Sleeveless

It didn't matter if it were summer or winter: women went sleeveless. Sleeveless dresses and blouses were comfortable because they allowed the shoulders to move freely. Women added stoles, or wraps, around their shoulders for casual and formal occasions. Stoles could be made of any material from the lightest chiffons to warm wool and even mink.

Silhouettes designed to flatter Junior Figures

[A] $8.54 [B] $10.74
Softer Looking Slim Dresses with New Details

[A] **Jumper Sheath** in deep-pile twill-back cotton velvet . . so flattering with its wide-scooped neck, front and back. Slim skirt has back kick pleat topped by a neat bow; 2 side seam pockets; back zipper. Wear alone or with blouses. Hand washable. Shpg. wt. 1 lb. 10 oz. *Order correct size. Juniors' sizes 9, 11, 13, 15, 17.*
031 D 5012—Black. $8.54
031 D 5013—Red. 8.54

[C] **Dressmaker Detailed** dress . . tiny dots on soft, lustrous Chromspun acetate taffeta. Empire bodice has deep folds, gros-grain band accents. Bill . . .

[B] **Softened Slim Dress** in c wool flannel. Wide-scoop neck, front and back; matchi rayon satin cummerbund, buckl in back. Tiny pleats give new e to skirt front. Back zipper, k pleat. Dry clean. Wt. 1 lb. 8 *Measure: please order correct s Juniors' sizes 7, 9, 11, 13, 15.*
031 D 6140—Navy blue. . . $10?
031 D 6141—Light blue. . . 10
031 D 6142—Lt. jade green 10

[D] **Full-skirted Date Dress** in s ly glowing acetate woven w a raised st . . . el-neckline . . . Sleeves h . . . ons-rea . . . Long b . . . t. 1 lb. 8 . . . correct s . . . 11, 13, 1 . . . .$10 . . . with l $1

[C] $14.70
Charming Bouffant S . . .
. . . the . . .

An alternative to the bouncy full skirt was the slim pencil skirt. It hugged the hips instead of hiding them. Pencil skirts look hard to walk around in, but they had small slits in the front or a longer one in the back for freedom of movement.

Introduction: Wild and Crazy Fads

Pull It All In

The latest fashions emphasized tiny waists. To help women with that, there were corsets. Corsets had stiff bones or hard plastic that squeezed the middle of the body. It was a relief to take them off at night.

But they did their job. In fact, they did it so well that they—and some of the dresses with built-in corsets—could stand up on their own.

A Pretty Picture

Picture a pencil. It's long and narrow, like one type of skirt that was popular in the 1950s. That's why it was called a pencil skirt. The pencil skirt came down straight to the knees, hugging a woman's body. Because it's tight, many pencil skirts had a back slit or pleat to give women room to walk.

Dorothy Dandridge (1922–1965), an American actress and singer, wore short, soft curls in 1954, a look that was both practical and glamorous.

Chapter 1

Hairstyles

By the 1950s, many women had given up their factory jobs. They also gave up the protective scarves that covered their heads. Now they had a chance to show off their hair! They cut and curled it. They slept in rollers. They got permanent waves. No one wanted long, straight hair. This was the time of soft and feminine hair. Women were ready to do anything they needed in order to get it.

There were no handheld blow-dryers, as we know them today. They were bulky models with hoses connected to plastic bonnets. Women also went to salons where they could sit under large domes that sent out hot air. Luckily, there were plenty of hair products on the market. These included home perms, curlers, hair spray, and gels. They allowed women to style their hair at home, often in their kitchens with funny-smelling chemicals!

FABULOUS FASHIONS of the 1950s

Ponytails

The ponytail was one of the most popular hairstyles in the 1950s. It was a simple, finished look that women could get by just pulling their hair back in elastic bands. The fifties' ponytails were usually pulled high up on the head. Bangs and curls provided additional interest. Many women tied scarves or ribbons around the bands. The ponytail was a more casual daytime look and not usually worn for fancy occasions.

Bouffant

There was no question about it: the bouffant was a glamorous hairstyle. Hair was first curled in large rollers. Then it was teased and combed high up on the head. Once enough height was reached, you pinned the hair in place and sprayed it. The bouffant style worked best with short to medium-length hair.

Poodle Cut

Short was "in" during the 1950s, and there's no better example than the poodle cut. Like its namesake, the cut was short and curly. Many women had to get a perm for this style. One of the most famous people to wear this cut was television star Lucille Ball. Women across the nation followed suit once they saw her with the poodle cut.

Lucille Ball (1911–1989) starred in the sitcom *I Love Lucy* as Lucy Ricardo alongside her real-life husband Desi Arnaz, who played Ricky Ricardo. Ball's poodle cut became an iconic hairstyle of the 1950s, but her influence on pop culture has lasted way beyond that decade. The show is still enjoyed by modern TV audiences, and many of the characters' funny stunts and mannerisms are often copied.

The Pompadour and Ducktail

Women weren't the only ones who had fun with their hair. Men in the fifties wore a variety of styles. Two popular ones were the ducktail and the pompadour. Both needed a lot of hair grease to stay in place.

FABULOUS FASHIONS of the 1950s

With the ducktail, men greased their hair and combed the sides back until they met in the middle. With the end of a comb, they made a center part down the back.

With the pompadour, men combed back the sides and greased them in place. Then they put the rest of the grease in the top of their hair. They combed it up to give it some height and smoothed it back. Sometimes they would leave a little curl on the side of the forehead.

Elvis Presley (1935–1977) was just as famous for his pompadour as he was for his hip swinging! The girls swooned over him, and young men all around the world copied his slick rock-and-roll style.

Chapter 2
Women's Styles and Fashion

Think about the shape of an hourglass. That was the shape that women's clothes created back in the fifties. Even the undergarments were designed for curves. Corsets made tiny waists even tinier and hips seem curvier. They may not have been comfortable, but women got used to them.

This was the new look for the fifties. It was much more feminine than the utility look of the past decade. Best of all, you could use as much material and decoration as you liked. The war was over, and material was available.

Styles fell into two categories—full or fitted. There were full skirts with lots of crinoline. There were formfitting skirts under suits with jackets nipped in at the waist.

This became the fifties look. If you were a 1950s woman or teen, you dressed this way. If you were unsure about what to wear, a skirt was always a safe bet.

It would not be until the end of the decade that women traded in their skirts for tight-fitting pants. It would become a time to experiment, and fashion was all the better for it.

Full of Fun!

Skirts were full in the fifties, helped by layers and layers of petticoats underneath. Sometimes women dipped the petticoats in a sugar solution to stiffen them. The skirts were usually worn with formfitting tops.

One fun version of the fifties full skirt was the poodle skirt. These skirts were popular with teenage girls, who often wore them to dances. They were often pink and featured a cute appliqué. This could be a poodle or something else, such as a flower or flamingo. Sometimes the design was studded with sequins or sparkles.

One Style Fits All

The chemise dress was easy for anyone to wear, no matter what her figure. This straight-cut dress had no real waist. Women created their own with belts. They could make it high, low, loose, or tight. The chemise could be used for casual or dressy wear, depending on what material was used. It could have sleeves or be sleeveless.

Two teenage girls work on a prom dress with a full skirt and tight bodice. Big, poofy skirts accentuated tiny waists to achieve hourglass figures. It was probably hard to sit down with all that crinoline underneath!

Push Those Pedals

The Italian motor scooter was an easy way to get around, but full skirts could easily get caught in its wheels. So women wore short capri-length pants called pedal pushers that fit close to the leg. They accessorized with scarves around their necks or over their short hair.

17

CAPRI PANTS . . the fun fashion of our times

Lean and leggy, they take leisure in their stride

A Stretchable Lastex® yarn combines with cotton to do wonderful, curve-controlling things for your figure. Back zipper. Hand washable. *State Misses'* size 10, 12, 14, 16, 18. Wt. 13 oz. T7 G 6456—Bright blue, green, brown......$5.97

B Fine Cotton Knit completely lined for shape retention and a smooth sleek fit. Back zipper closing. Hand washable. *Misses'* sizes 10, 12, 14, 16, 18. *State size.* Shipping wt. 13 oz. T7 G 6044—Black. $4.87

C Paisley Corduroy shows a flair for the exotic. Tapered legs slit at side. Back zipper. Hand wash separately. *Misses'* sizes 10, 12, 14, 16, 18. *State size.* Shipping wt. 13 oz. T7 G 6454—Red, green and blue print.....$4.97

D Lustrous Sateen . . fine combed cotton tailored smartly high-rise waist, self belt, side pocket and side zipper. Washable. *State Misses'* size 10, 12, 14, 16, 18. Wt. 13 oz. T7 G 6463—Star sapphire blue...............$2.83 T7G6464—Black... 2.83 T7G6465—Lt. beige 2.83

E Striped Denim . . sturdy, rugged fabric now more fashionable than ever. Back zipper. Belt included. Washable. *State Misses'* size 10, 12, 14, 16, 18. Wt. 12 oz. T7 G 6475—Black, gray and gold stripe....$2.97 T7 G 6476—Wine red, gray and gold stripe $2.97

F Ribbed Cotton Cord. An adjustable D-ring waist and slant pockets define a smart look in sportswear. Back zipper closing. Washable. *State Misses'* size 10, 12, 14, 16, 18. Wt. 12 oz. T7 G 6470—Ruby red T7 G 6471—Black T7 G 6472—Deep beige Each...............$3.77

G Checked Corduroy pays dividends in fun fashion. Leather-gold-color

C $4.97

B $4.87

A $5.97

G $4.77 Pants

H $2.83 Pullover

The terms *pedal pushers* and *capri pants* are used interchangeably to describe close-fitting pants that end above the ankle. They were more comfortable and practical than full skirts and tight pencil skirts but just as fashionable!

18

Beatnik Style

There were people who rebelled against the "living doll" fashion and the gray flannel suit. They were known as beatniks. Beatniks would gather in cafés, have poetry readings, and listen to jazz.

The beatnik fashion was untraditional, too. Women wore black turtlenecks or long heavy sweaters over tight fitting pants. Sometimes they wore black skirts and tights. Ballet flats finished the look.

Ahead of Her Time

Some of today's fashions were created by designer Bonnie Cashin back in the 1950s. Do you have a roomy turtleneck that you can pull over you head? Do you wear layers of clothing? Do you own a tote bag? Those and more are thanks to Bonnie Cashin. They were all created with the modern woman in mind.

Blonde Bombshell

With her hourglass figure and pouty mouth, Marilyn Monroe was the blonde bombshell of the 1950s. She was one of the most successful actresses then—and remains famous today long after her death. Fans copied her fashions, such as the billowy white halter dress she wore in her movie *The Seven Year Itch*.

This photograph of Marilyn Monroe (1926–1962) was taken September 9, 1954, in New York City over a subway grating. This flirty pose has become an iconic image in American pop culture. Marilyn Monroe was born Norma Jeane Mortenson, and she was actually a brunette!

Going Glam

When you think of glamorous evening-wear, think of French designer Pierre Balmain. He designed elegant gowns with tight bodices and full skirts. His short cocktail dresses were embroidered in satin and velvet.

His designs were so popular that they appeared in more than seventy films of the time. Balmain also designed for the queen of Thailand and film stars Marlene Dietrich and Vivien Leigh.

Chapter 3

Men's Styles and Fashion

While women had many choices in what to wear, men did not. Most men looked the same going to work each day, wearing their gray flannel suits.

That didn't mean that men only wore suits. Men's cardigans were also popular. These are sweaters that button up the front. Cardigans were more casual, but they still looked neat.

Teenagers wore outfits similar to the gray flannel suits of their fathers. They might have worn just the shirt and pants or added a jacket or cardigan. Ties came out for more formal occasions.

But not everyone dressed this way. Some younger men rebelled. The greasers preferred a more casual style, including jeans. Much of their style is still popular today.

The Man in the Gray Flannel Suit

The gray flannel suit was single-breasted. It had a jacket that overlapped only enough for a single row of buttons. Men wore the suit with a white shirt and a silk tie. They wore it in all seasons, during hot and cold weather. After work, men would relax in their gray flannel suits after removing their ties.

Gregory Peck (1916–2003) starred in the 1956 film *The Man in the Gray Flannel Suit*. The gray flannel suit became a sort of uniform for middle-class businessmen. It was more than just an outfit. It came to symbolize corporate America.

No Better Sweater

Cardigan sweaters had been popular with college men since the 1920s. They became even more popular during the 1950s. Cardigans were comfortable alternatives to suit jackets and vests. The cardigans were more casual but still had a polished look. Men wore them over a shirt and pants for added warmth and style.

Grease It Back

Forget the suit. Put away the cardigan. The greasers are here! This group was named for the large amount of hair grease that they used. The greasers wore white or black T-shirts, jeans, leather jackets, and boots. They were rebels who used fashion to express themselves. We call them greasers today, but in the 1950s, they were known as "hoods."

Not Just for Cowboys

The movies of the time also influenced fashion. Cowboys were already wearing jeans in films, but it wasn't until top movie stars wore them that the style took off. Marlon Brando played an outlaw biker in *The Wild One.* He wore jeans. James Dean played the lead role in *Rebel Without a Cause,* also in jeans.

The movies had a real effect on the men of the time. Younger men started to wear jeans for casual wear. Older men wore them in the same way the cowboys did—only when they were going to get sweaty and messy.

Set-ups...

Imported Shell Cordovans

New from England! . . finest cordovan leather. Fully leather lined. Double leather sole, leather heel with metal V-plate.

Sizes: B (narrow) 9 to 11, 12, 13.
Sizes: C (med. narrow) 8 to 11, 12.
Sizes: D (medium) 7 to 11, 12, 13.

Half sizes too (no 11½, 12½).
State size, width. Wt. 2 lbs. 8 oz.
T 67F4447A—Cordovan.Pr .$14.90
T 67 F 4448A—Black . .Pair 14.90

Set-up for style and warmth

100% Lamb's Wool Coat-Sweater. Button-front. Shawl collar. Hand washable. *State size* small (36–38-in. chest), medium (40–42), large (44–46). See measuring instructions on page 699. Shipping weight 1 pound 8 ounces.
33 F 2200—Black   33 F 2201—Light Oxford gray
33 F 2202—Dark Brown . . . . .Each $8.90

Bulky-knit Combed Cotton Crew Socks. Striped! Moroul® elastic top. Washfast. *State color* black or brown.
10½, 11, 11½, 12, 13.   Pair 87c

The defining characteristic of a cardigan sweater (right) is its open front. It can have buttons, zippers, or ties down the center.

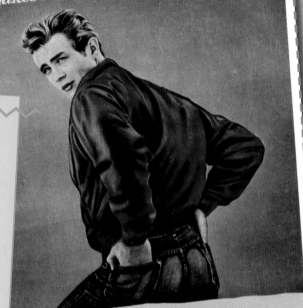

A movie poster for *Rebel Without a Cause*. James Dean (1931–1955) plays a rebellious teenager struggling to get along with his parents and dealing with bullies at his high school. He personified the "bad boy" image with his tough-guy attitude and carefree style.

Chapter 4

Accessories

You probably just wear gloves in the winter when it's cold. In the 1950s, women wore them to dress up. It was one of the accessories that every lady had to have. Gloves were made of cotton or the new nylon. White and cream were the most popular colors.

Gloves were so popular that the purses of the time included side pockets or rings. That was where women could put their gloves when they weren't wearing them.

Shoes were another main accessory. Unlike the previous decade, there were lots of choices. Women's shoes were very feminine and came in pretty colors with high heels. Styles were plentiful. The more comfortable saddle shoes were a favorite of teenagers.

The Bell Silhouette, young and sophisticated, charmingly fashioned in crisp acetate taffeta. Low rounded neckline in back; long back zipper. Pleats and cuff all around skirt; 2-inch hem. The new tapered skirt is wide enough for walking. Dry clean. Jewelry sold in Jewelry Section.
Misses' sizes 10, 12, 14, 16, 18, 20. *State size.* Shpg. wt. 1 lb.
T 31 G 5350—Peacock blue, green, black paisley print . . $9.50

The Harem Skirted Dress, curving in and under to accentuate the long-legged look. Here in a winter-blooming print of billowing rayon and acetate taffeta. All-around midriff; acetate velvet belt. Deep V neckline and long zipper in back. Dress is lined from midriff to hem. Dry clean. Shipping weight 1 pound 12 ounces.
Fits Juniors and Misses . . . State size 7-8, 9-10, 11-12, 13-14, 15-16.
T 31 G 7203—Autumn gold and brown on bla[...]
T 31 G 7204—Sapphire (medium) [...]
on black.

The Feather Clip is a Siren, all hand-curled feathers and devastating charm. So easy to wear, it clasps your curls with a side-wise curve, fits all head sizes. *State color* . . . sapphire blue (medium), white, red, black, or light pink.
T 78 G 6705—Shpg. wt. 8 o[...]

The Elegant [...]

Jewelry Tailored splendor. Crystal rhinestone baguettes. Necklace adjusts to 16½ in. ⅞ in. earrings. *State gold or silver color.* Wt. 3 oz.
4G3738E—Necklace, earrings [...]
4G3739E—Necklace, earrings $4[...]
4G3[...]

Rayon Satin Clutch has a 24K gold-plated frame. Rayon lining and coin purse. Rayon [...]
191[...]

Accessorizing was a great way to make the same outfit look different! The feather clip added flair to your curly do. A rhinestone jewelry set made you sparkle. You could carry your personal items in a strapless purse called a clutch. Gloves and high heels completed your sophisticated look.

Hats were not the important accessories that they were in past times. Women wore them more at the beginning of the decade than at the end.

Glasses, however, became a new accessory. People had worn glasses for decades, but in the 1950s, they started to show some personal style.

The Height of Fashion

High heels were all the rage in the 1950s. They drew attention to women's ankles and calves. The style was to wear a very thin heel, made possible by Italian shoe designer Ferragamo. He was the first to put a steel support into a man-made heel.

The new stiletto heels drew notice from men and women everywhere, but that's not all.

fashion points

High, skinny heels lengthened and slimmed women's legs. They may not have been the most comfortable shoes, but they were definitely attention-grabbers! Most of the shoes featured here have 2¾-inch heels. That may not sound very high, but the thinness of the heel put more pressure on the balls of the feet.

Hotels and airports paid special attention. That was because the steel supports were making holes in their floors! Carpet was found to be one solution to the problem.

Saddle Up

While women wore heels, teenagers wore saddle shoes. You could find these shoes on the feet of both girls and boys in the 1950s.

Saddle shoes were white shoes with a black or brown piece of leather across the middle. It resembled a saddle, which is how the shoes were named. Saddle shoes were as common back then as sneakers are today.

For Eyes With Style

Spectacles, or glasses, were considered a glamorous accessory. People did not wear contacts back then. Anyone who needed to improve their vision reached for their glasses.

Sparkly spectacles from 1955. Notice the cat-eye shape and bejeweled frames.

Just as the styles of glasses change over time, the 1950s had its own look. For women, the tops of the spectacles flared out like butterfly wings or cat's eyes. They were often decorated with sparkles of some kind. For men, the style was black glasses with thicker and wider frames.

Heads Up!

In the early 1950s, women were still wearing hats. These were smaller versions, from the pillbox with a veil to the beret. Women wore the hats more toward the front of their heads.

As the decade went on, women stopped wearing as many hats. They spent so much time doing their hair that they didn't want hats to mess it up!

Chapter 5
Fads and Trends

It was trendy to be a teenager in the 1950s. Teenagers had more freedom than ever. Their parents, having gone through the Great Depression, wanted more for their children. They encouraged them to get jobs and to go to college. Parents allowed their teenagers to think for themselves.

That wasn't the only thing that was different about the 1950s. There were lots of new ideas. Artificial fabrics changed what people wore. These fabrics were produced in mass so everyone had access to them.

Black and white continued to be popular colors during this time. But the Spanish influence brought more vivid ones. It also brought the idea of a culture outside the United States that was affecting fashion.

The movie industry affected fashion as well, from the dresses of Doris Day to the coonskin caps of Davy Crockett.

Talk About Teens!

You know the word *teenager*. But before the 1950s, it did not exist. Younger children were girls and boys. Older children were youths. At age eighteen, they were adults.

Teenagers hang out at a diner to enjoy food and quality time with friends. Back then, you could've eaten a hamburger for forty-nine cents or breakfast for thirty cents! You also could've put a coin into a jukebox and chosen a song you wanted to hear. Many restaurants today still have jukeboxes, but they play digital files instead of records.

During the 1950s, that all changed. Teenagers had their own social lives, going to soda fountains, movies, and dances. They had their own values and lingo, which were very different from their parents' culture. Adults disapproved of almost every aspect of teenagers' lives, from their fashion to their music. Girls were not allowed to wear pants. Boys were not allowed to wear jeans in public or have haircuts that were long enough to touch their ears.

Rock and roll was born in the fifties and teens loved it! Parents saw how their kids lost control while listening to it, screaming, dancing, and sometimes, even fainting. They viewed it as immoral and dangerous, but it was here to stay!

Made in the Lab

Due to scientific advancements, there were plenty of man-made fabrics in the 1950s. These fabrics changed how clothes looked and felt. For one thing, they weighed less. They also required less care.

Nylon had been used for stockings. Now it was also being used for everything from underwear to fake fur. It could be produced in a heavyweight or lightweight form. Dacron® was another man-made material. It did not wrinkle but could hold permanent creases.

Nylon and Dacron were easy to wash, quick to dry, and did not shrink. Both men and women replaced their wool knits and cottons with these new materials.

Our Lowest Price Ever!

COOL COTTON and DACRON* DRESSES

A smash hit in this summery lightweight fabric . . laboratory
tested to wash, keep its color, resist perspiration stains
SALE ENDS AUGUST 17th

$7.00 Each

[A] ...waist . . sizes

[B] **Tucked-Front Dress . .** sizes 7 to 15. A wonderful ...pastel colors

[C] **V-Neck Dress . .** sizes 12 to 20. A feminine, full-skirted dress with smart V neckline in back. The silk ...th orna-...Flower ...ds little ...lb. 4 oz. ...t. ..16, 18, ...oise and ....$7.00 ...rose and ....$7.00 ...and black $7.00

[D] **Tab-Trimmed Dress . .** sizes 12 to 20; 14½ to 24½. Well made, youthful dress has hip pocket detail, slim skirt with back kick pleat, back zipper. White linen-look rayon trim and silk square. Washable. Shpg. wt. 1 lb. 4 oz. *Misses' sizes* 12, 14, 16, 18, 20; *Half sizes* 14½, 16½, 18½, 20½, 22½, 24½. *Order correct size.*
031 J 3411—Light blue
031 J 3412—Pale green
031 J 3413—Light lilac
Each $7.00

*DuPont T. M. for polyester fiber

In addition to being wrinkle-free, these Dacron dresses also promise to keep their color in the wash and resist sweat stains. It made laundry a lot easier for the average housewife!

FABULOUS FASHIONS of the 1950s

A Touch of Spain

Bullfighters were popular in Spain, and their fashion was popular in the United States. The matador, or bullfighter, wears a certain type of hat and jacket. Designers offered matador hats and bolero jackets in rich colors from yellow to red and black. Fringe was frequently used in these designs.

American actress and singer Eartha Kitt (1927–2008) dons a short-sleeved, white bolero jacket in the 1958 movie *Anna Lucasta*.

Furry Nice!

In 1955, Walt Disney introduced *Davy Crockett, King of the Wild Frontier.* This American folk hero fought for justice with a rifle named Old Betsy. But it was his coonskin cap, complete with raccoon tail, that attracted the most attention.

The cap was so popular that children throughout the United States were caught up in the fad. Some reports said that the movie made more money in merchandise than it did at the box office!

Chapter 6

Pop Culture

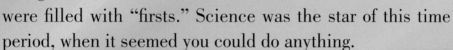

The first rocket in space, the first leak-free ballpoint pen, the first credit card, a television set in your living room . . . the 1950s were filled with "firsts." Science was the star of this time period, when it seemed you could do anything.

Americans saw the space race begin. The first rocket launches were broadcast on television! The United States and the Soviet Union battled to get satellites into orbit.

Meanwhile, back on earth, Americans discovered rock and roll. The new music idols also had a lot to do with fashion. Men copied the styles of Elvis Presley, Bill Hayley, Jerry Lee Lewis, Chuck Berry, and Little Richard.

Boys wore narrow ties and jackets or adopted the greaser look with black leather jackets over T-shirts. Girls danced in billowing circle skirts, bobby socks, and saddle shoes.

Some wore sheer blouses with pretty slips underneath. Fashion even made it into the songs of the time, such as Elvis Presley's hit "Blue Suede Shoes."

It's TV Time!

Forget the flat-screen color TVs in your living room. The first television sets were large pieces of furniture that broadcast only in black and white. Even so, if you had a TV in your home in 1950, you would be the most popular kid on the block. By 1954, about one in every seven people owned a TV set.

There were not many channels available. Only three networks existed: NBC, ABC, and CBS. But they offered something for everyone.

Kids watched *Howdy Doody Time, Lassie, The Mickey Mouse Club*, and *American Bandstand*. Other favorite shows of the time included *I Love Lucy, The Honeymooners, The Twilight Zone*, and *Adventures of Superman*.

Rock Around the Clock

Americans started to swing to a whole new sound in the 1950s—rock and roll. This type of music really caught on with the teenagers. They swooned to Elvis; danced to Chuck Berry; and shook, rattled, and rolled to Big Joe Turner.

A family gathers around to watch their favorite program. Television gave families another way to spend time together. Many TV shows from the 1950s, such as *Lassie*, *The Twilight Zone*, and *Superman*, were remade in later decades.

The afternoon television program *American Bandstand* showcased the new rock and roll. It also launched the careers of many performers, from its host Dick Clark to Bill Haley and the Comets, Bobby Darin, and Fabian.

Dick Clark (center) hosted *American Bandstand* from 1956 to 1989. The program showed teenagers dancing to the hit music of the day. Music channels like MTV and VH1 have *American Bandstand* to thank for making music television featuring young people popular!

Let's Go to the Hop!

If your school is like the ones back in the 1950s, your dances are probably held in the gym. The teenagers back then used to kick off their shoes. They were more easily able to slide to dances like the Twist or the Mashed Potato. Not only was it more fun to dance that way, they wouldn't mark up the gym floor with shoe marks.

Someone called one of these dances "a sock hop" and it stuck. There were several songs written about it. "At the Hop," one of the most popular, was done by Danny and the Juniors.

Get Ready to Hula!

Coles Department Store sold the first plastic hoops in 1957. But the hula-hoop really took off the following year when Wham-O made them and sold more than 100 million! There were contests throughout the United States that judged you on how many hoops you could twirl, how long you could hula-hoop, and even on fancy moves like the knee knocker or stork. Hula-hoops continue to be popular today. All you need is some space and a wiggle in your hips!

Children, two to sixteen years old, compete in a hula hoop contest in Los Angeles on August 20, 1958.

Timeline

(The) 1920s

The look: cloche hats, dropped-waist dresses, long strands of pearls (women), and baggy pants (men)

The hair: short bobs

The fad: raccoon coats

(The) 1930s

The look: dropped hemlines, natural waists, practical shoes (women), and blazers and trousers (men)

The hair: finger waves and permanents

The fad: sunbathing

(The) 1940s

The look: shirtwaist dresses and military style (women) and suits and fedoras (men)

The hair: victory rolls and updos

The fad: kangaroo cloaks

The 1950s

The look: circular skirts and saddle shoes (women) and
the greaser look (men)

The hair: bouffants and pompadours

The fad: coonskin caps

The 1960s

The look: bell-bottoms and miniskirts (women) and
turtlenecks and hipster pants (men)

The hair: beehives and pageboys

The fad: go-go boots

The 1970s

The look: designer jeans (women) and leisure suits (men)

The hair: shags and Afros

The fad: hot pants

The 1980s

The look: preppy (women and men) and *Miami Vice* (men)

The hair: side ponytails and mullets

The fad: ripped off-the-shoulder sweatshirts

The 1990s

The look: low-rise, straight-leg jeans (both women and men)

The hair: the "Rachel" cut from *Friends*

The fad: ripped, acid-washed jeans

The 2000s

The look: leggings and long tunic tops (women) and the sophisticated urban look (men)

The hair: feminine, face-framing cuts (with straight hair dominating over curly)

The fad: organic and bamboo clothing

Glossary

accessories—Items that are not part of your main clothing but worn with it, such as jewelry, gloves, hats, and belts.

beatnik—A person who rebelled against the conventional society of the 1950s, emphasized artistic expression, and usually dressed all in black.

capri—Calf-length women's pants.

cardigan—A type of sweater that opens in the front.

corset—A woman's tight-fitting, boned undergarment used to squeeze in the waist.

crinoline—A stiff fabric that is used underneath skirts to fluff them up.

fad—A craze that happens for a brief period of time.

fashion—The current style of dressing.

greaser—A rebellious young man from the 1950s, usually of the working class, who dressed in T-shirts, leather jackets, and jeans and slicked his hair back.

merchandise—The items that we buy.

pedal pushers—Another term for capri pants.

petticoats—Underskirts that are often trimmed with ruffles or lace.

rebel—Someone who goes against the established society.

stilettos—Thin, spiked, high-heeled shoes.

stole—A long, wide piece of fabric, often made of chiffon, wool, or fur, worn across the shoulders.

trend—The general direction in which things are heading.

vivid—Intensely bright.

Further Reading

Books

Baker, Patricia. *Fashions of a Decade: The 1950s*. New York: Facts On File, 2006.

Jones, Jen. *Fashion History: Looking Great Through the Ages*. Mankato, Minn.: Capstone Press, 2007.

Lindop, Edmund, and Sarah De Capua. *America in the 1950s*. Minneapolis, Minn.: Twenty-First Century Books, 2009.

Rooney, Anne. *The 1950s and 1960s*. New York: Chelsea House, 2009.

Internet Addresses

Fashion-Era, "1950s Fashion Glamour"
<http://www.fashion-era.com/1950s_glamour.htm>

1950s Fashion
<http://www.challengefashion.com/>

Index

A

accessories, 27–31
American Bandstand, 39, 40

B

Ball, Lucille, 12, 13
Balmain, Pierre, 21
beatnik, 19
blow-dryer, 11
bobby socks, 37
bolero, 36
bouffant, 12
Brandon, Marlon, 24
bullfighter, 36

C

capris (also see *pedal pushers*), 17, 18
cardigan, 22, 24, 25
Cashin, Bonnie, 19
chemise, 16
Clark, Dick, 39, 40
coonskin cap, 36
corset, 9
cowboy, 24
Crockett, Davy, 32, 36
curls, 10, 11, 12

D

Dacron, 34, 35
Dandridge, Dorothy, 10
Dean, James, 24, 26
ducktail, 13, 14
dungarees, 17

F

fitted style, 5, 9, 15
full style, 5, 15, 16, 17, 18

G

glasses, 29–31
gloves, 7, 27
gray flannel suit, 22, 23
greaser, 24, 37
Great Depression, 32

H

hats, 7, 29, 31, 36
hourglass figure, 15, 17, 20
housewife, 5, 35
hula-hoops, 41

I

I Love Lucy, 13

J

jeans, 17, 24, 34

K

Kelly, Grace, 6
Kitt, Eartha, 36

M

Monroe, Marilyn, 20
Mortenson, Norma Jeane, 20
motor scooter, 17

N

nylon, 27, 34

P

pants, 7, 16, 17, 19, 22, 24, 34
Peck, Gregory, 23
pedal pushers, 17, 18
pencil skirt, 5, 9, 18
permanents, 11, 12
petticoat, 5, 16
pompadour, 13, 14
ponytail, 12
poodle cut, 12
poodle skirt, 16
Presley, Elvis, 14, 37, 38

R

Rebel Without a Cause, 24, 26
rock and roll, 34, 37, 38, 39

S

saddle shoes, 28, 30, 37
sheer blouses, 5, 38
slips, 5, 38
sock hop, 40
space race, 37
Spain, 36
stiletto heels, 29
stole, 6, 7

T

teenager, 5, 16, 17, 27, 32–34
television, 5, 12, 37, 38, 39, 40
turtleneck, 19

U

undergarments, 15
utility look, 15